IN ANOTHER COUNTRY

Pray for Joy

Rafiq Kathwari

Rafiq

January 2025

Doire Press

First published in September 2015

Doire Press
Aille, Inverin
Co. Galway
www.doirepress.com

Layout: Lisa Frank
Front cover design: Masood Hussain & Farah Brigante
Cover image: *Back to the Roots* by Masood Hussain
Painting in mixed medium, 48" X 48", 2011
Private collection of Delhi Public School, Athwajan, Srinagar, Kashmir
Author photo: Mohammad Tabish

Printed by Clódóirí CL
Casla, Co. na Gaillimhe

ISBN 978-1-907682-40-7

We gratefully acknowledge the assistance of The Arts Council / An Chomhairle Ealaíon.

For my mother, Maryam

CONTENTS

Much madness is divinest sense —

Emily Dickinson

What Happened to a World

My mother cross-legged
on the verandah rug
scent of mustard oil
her glistening hair
fat cook on bike
midday tiffin to Father

I open my jaw to Maa
purse my lips to moo
fleece white as snow on K2
bathe my lamb Maamoo
in an oval tin tub
under the grand oak

Eid al-Adha
day of sacrifice
the cook ropes Maamoo's legs
Mother pulls at her hair
pleading with Father
knife at Maamoo's throat

In the name of Allah
Father's *Bismillah*
blood crescent soaking grass
Mamoo's head at my feet
eyes reflecting light
of dead stars

Hallucinations

for Richard Howard

The servants never listen to me
only when the new wife nods
they run around like rats
to fetch the thermos

there is poison in the spring water
Chanel!
a present from my son Farooq
in America — the wind

carried my message
after all
thieves
        under my bed

I want latches on my door
and a mirror
the old one shattered
when the nail

gave way
I hang my shawl on the wall
dried roses upside down
my room not swept for six days

no water to
soak clothes
my daughter will clean
        when she visits

the door is bolted
from outside
if the house catches fire who will
open it?

Will I burn alive?
The servants' outhouse
                        turns my stomach
a pane is broken

I'll spray Chanel!
My grandson from his grave
come to visit
he is with his great-grandfather

they both received transfusions
my husband says I don't need a doctor
but that doesn't keep his new wife
from going to Combined Hospital

I am still the head of this household
O Wind
         tell my son in America
the dollars he sends

the new wife misspends
tell him I need a car
to buy roses
at Shalimar

my husband has lost interest
in roses
for years he's been saying
Maryam is mad, mad

Is there anything wrong with me?
My sky is vaster than my mind
my son builds homes for me
                        in America

views of river and rolling hills
the Maharaja of Kashmir exhales —
no water
       I have no water

the servant washing dishes
keeps it from reaching me
everyone has cancer
including the midwives

O North Wind
what is taking my grandson so long?
Dead mosquitoes
              in my denture bowl

Lost in Translation

"I have a radio in my head
and I'm forever listening

to whispers, always whispers,"
Mother tells Harry the shrink,

who puts a rubber band on her arm,
and flicks it. "Did that turn

off the radio?" he asks.
She winces, removes the band.

"You've made this into child's play,"
she says, swiveling her chair

to glare at me, her fifth child,
reclined on the couch

translating Urdu,
Mother tongue.

My Parents' Nuptials

for Colette Inez

As arranged, they meet the first time.
He's a law student. She's a child-bride.

She wears red: for rancour?
Head bowed, veiled little stars

in gold thread, waits on the bed
like an arrow drawn on a bow.

Henna-touched hands, a mirror poised
on lap: a girl staring back.

If he sits beside her,
she will see him glance at her image.

In the courtyard, children sing,
"Petals fall from almond trees."

The singing could continue until
he displays a blood-stained sheet.

Footfalls on stairs, whispers,
robes rustling, attar of roses.

His hand on her chin, her heart leaping.
He kisses her eyes closed.

"Stop. Sever the bond," I scream,
"He'll play possum, make you prey."

The mirror slips from her fingers,
bangles clash on her fleshy arms.

Sunday Bath

for Gerald Jonas

My sister latched the door:
a tube of light through the pane
shocked the cement floor.

My kid brother and I sat
naked near a bucket,
a canister to scoop water.

Lifebuoy soap on chipped saucer,
a cylindrical container poised on bricks,
a tap crudely soldered to its hem.

Under the container,
nuggets glowed on a charcoal burner
heating up the water.

Let's be clear about this: no
shower, no tub, no sink, no mirror,
only a hole in the floor

for draining waste bath water out to a gully.
To be fair to bathrooms he had known,
Father had named it The Cube.

Dizzy and nauseous, heart faster,
beads of sweat on bony chest,
the more I breathed, the more I gasped,

wondering what was taking my sister
so long to scoop water from the bucket
and shower it on my head.

She dragged herself to the door
on tip-toe to reach the latch, fell back,
slowly rose, her fingers clawing the pane.

My kid brother collapsed
on the floor, his mouth an O.
Are we playing dead?

Charcoal, the Mother of All Coals,
Father later said, burns quickly
in airtight rooms, releases deadly gas.

You can't see, smell, or taste it.
Inhaled, it displaces oxygen
we breathe to stay alive.

I remember only blurs: glass
shattering, treetops waving, sirens,
a cold mask on my face: breathing.

Farooq, older brother, waiting
his turn to bathe, sat on a small
crate outside the Cube, reading

Superman, wondered
why no waste water flowed
out to the open gully

in the courtyard. He bolted upstairs
to tell Father, who ran down
without touching the handrail,

broke the pane, unlatched the door,
dragged us all out, and sent Farooq
on his Hero bike to summon the Red Cross.

My sister gradually grew
protective of me and my kid brother
who stopped sucking his thumb, after all.

Praised for his presence of mind,
Farooq promised but never gave me his comics
and never lets us forget his heroics.

Seeing her three angels in mortal poses,
Mother ripped her blouse,
pummeled her bosom. "There is no god

but God, no god but God, no god."
The next day, my parents sacrificed
a lamb, gave meat to other refugees

camped in Muzzaffarabad
near the Cease-Fire Line,
after the first war over Kashmir.

In Another Country

for Agha Shahid Ali

In Kashmir, half-asleep, Mother listens to the rain.
In Manhattan, I feel her presence in the rain.

A rooster precedes the Call to Prayer at Dawn:
God is a namedropper: all names at once in the rain.

Forsythias shrivel in a glass vase on her nightstand.
On my windowsills, wilted petals, a petulance in the rain.

She must wonder when I will put on the kettle,
butter the crumpets, observe silence in the rain.

She veils her hair, offers a prayer across the oceans,
water on my hands becomes a reverence in the rain.

At Jewel House in Srinagar, Mother reshapes my *ghazal.*
"No enjambments!" she says as I listen in the rain.

"Rafiq," I hear her call above the city din.
The kettle whistles: Mother's scent in the rain.

Yeti Yanks the Crazy-Quilt

"You are a prophet. You are."
She mimics cock-a-doodle-do.

A Lord of the Skies booms
the Himalayas. She dashes

to the window screaming,
"Firewood up yours,"

her fist blossoming, returns
to her bed where her yeti

yanks the crazy-quilt over
her head like a tea-cosy.

Curled up on my straw mattress
on the hard floor, I watch

an astounded rooster beating
his wings against the pane.

House Call

"Smoothen moonbeams back into my throat,"
she pleads with a god in tails.
An angel straps her ankles,
pads her temples,
shoves a rag in her mouth,
pins her fleshy arms,
kisses her eyes closed.

God in tails flicks on his volt box.
Bulbs flicker. She sizzles.
Cold full moon of Kashmir
discovers her attic room
where a boy, birthmark on forehead,
tip-toes to his mother's bed.
She calmly asks me my name.

Late Retort

"Fire log in cunt,"
a pious father yells
at his daughter —

> *Now this sounds authentic*
> *but would a Kashmiri father*
> *use this word? Few would*
> *in the West. Few do in the East.*
> *But this isn't fiction.*

— who tells him
an egg she swallowed
has grown a chick
inside her belly.

Certain his only child is possessed,
he buys a perky hen
to entice the chick and purge it.
Hen flutters in his hands
as he chases his daughter
barefoot around their backyard
a day after snow.

The daughter lunges
like a snow hare
into the snowbank
to outrun her fuming father.

Three score and three years later,
she plumbs a memory,
summons all her frail strength
to yell, "Fire log in prick,"
back at her long-deceased father,
who she insists in a shrill voice

is alive at her childhood home
in Kashmir. At Farooq's home
in New Rochelle,
in my usual heartless way
I administer two pills,
Ativan and *Zyprexa*,
to chill Mother's mind.

A Resurrection

My mother tells this story
about her childhood in Kashmir,
years before she married my father.

"I remember our horse Burak,
hoofs scuffing snow, nostrils fuming,
hitched to an open cart. Relatives

showering rice and rose petals
on Mohammed's shrouded body —
the son my father always wanted

to whom I was betrothed,
wailed not for a soul departed
but sang of a bride awaiting

an intended groom
who succumbed
to the Mother Of Chills."

Three score and four years later,
Mother rises from the bright
Ethan Allen tight-back couch

at Farooq's home in New Rochelle
to do what she does best now
— merging time past and time present —

whispers across Long Island Sound,
"Mohammed,
have they given you a transfusion?"

Motherboard

if only i could
redraw her map
revamp her amps
rebuild her microchips
resize her conduits
rift her polarities
ring her circuits
repulse her impulses
raise her thresholds
recess her receptors
rewrite her scripts
retrace her synapses
recall her memories
i would regain Mother

I Translate, from the Urdu, Mother's Dream for Harry the Shrink

Naked,
except for my nikab,

roped to a round pillar
on a sand dune

the sun's anvil,
my feet dancing.

The turbaned Bedouin,
henna-dyed beard,

Champion Lovemaker
peace be upon Him

raked His fingers at me.
Quicksand rose to my thighs.

My heart sank.
I awoke.

       Harry the shrink turns towards me
       and says, "Repressed sexual fantasy,

       need for intimacy.
       Nakedness: vulnerability;

       nikab veiling her face
       below the eyes: anonymity.

       Bondage suggests either
       a desire to be submissive, or

a yearning to be free.
Sinking into quicksand:

reversion into the subconscious.
Guilt about her desires

drives her to religion —
the *Champion Lovemaker* —

to rekindle her self esteem,
and make her feel better."

"What is he saying to you?" Mother asks.
"It's my dream, after all."

I resort to diplomacy. "Mother,
doctor sahib says I should help you

write down or tape record your dreams.
They are windows to your soul."

Mother's Scribe

Half-moon above the table
her face by candlelight

her upper lip twitches
my right leg flutters

In All Things Be Men
the school motto on my cap

Parker fountain pen
gold-plated nib

Waterman's ink
eggshell paper

my blue-black fingers
pilot her fervent verses

to prime ministers of the world
a moth at a candle's edge

flame flickering
only calligraphy at her robe's hem

Lines

6 July, 1956
General Dwight D Eisenhower,
Embassy of the United States,
Karachi. Dear Mr. President,
First of all, I wish you good luck

in your bid for re-election.
You're my president as well,
leader of all who seek freedom

from oppression of all hues.
America is a bulwark for liberty,
a terror for tyrants.
We Kashmiris want to be free.
I'm a mother. I hate false lines

rending sisters from brothers.
I wish to bring up all my children
together. Sadly, a Cease-Fire Line

divides my two older children
in Indian-occupied Kashmir,
from their younger four siblings
in Pakistan-occupied Kashmir.
Children who grow up apart

become strangers later in their lives.
It breaks my heart.
The nuns at Jesus and Mary Convent

in Murree easily cross the Line
to teach at the Presentation Convent
in Srinagar: Why can't my children?
Is Justice blind?
I urge you, Mr. President, command

one of your generals to bring
his tanks here to at once
re-unite Kashmir.

Our young men and women are prepared
to fight for their freedom.
We want the world to know our resolve.
Please help us air our determination
by printing this in *The New York Times.*

I pray for your victory in November.
Faithfully yours, Mrs. Maryam Jan,
"Katrina," Pindi Point, Murree.

Just Solution

Foreign Service of the United States
American Consulate General
Lahore, Pakistan, 20 August, 1956

        Mrs. Maryam Jan, Bungalow Katrina
        Pindi Point, Murree, Dear Mrs. Jan,

We acknowledge receipt of your recent letter
addressed to President Eisenhower.
Since you reside in this area, I have been

        asked to reply for the President. The United
        States Government is always glad to hear

various views concerning the very
important Kashmir question, and we found
your letter very interesting. You will

        understand, I am sure, the newspapers
        in the United States are not controlled

by the Government. We are therefore unable
to have your letter published in *The New York Times*.
You may be assured, however, the United

        States will continue to support a just
        solution to the Kashmir problem.

Thank you again for your letter. Very
truly yours, for the Consul General,
Robert P. Smith, American Vice Consul.

Ataturk

Turkish Embassy, Karachi
16 August, 1957

Mrs. Maryam Jan, "Katrina"
Pindi Point, Murree, West Pakistan

Dear Madam, I have received your letter.
Thank you very much for good wishes

expressed therein. I have pleasure
enclosing herewith a photograph

of Mustafa Kemal Ataturk,
as requested. Yours faithfully,

for Ambassador of Turkey
Ercument Yavuzalp, First Secretary.

Folk Women

His Excellency the Ambassador
Turkish Embassy, Karachi
17 April, 1958

Your Excellency, I am really sorry for the delay
acknowledging your letter of
16 August, 1957
            enclosed therewith photograph
of Mustafa Kemal Ataturk, who yanked
the women of Turkey
into the 20th century. In fact
            I wished to give you
the gift I promised in my last letter
personally on behalf
of myself and women folk of Kashmir
            during my anticipated
trip to Karachi. Sadly, I could not
travel so far. Hence, I am
sending the gift herewith, representing
            the handiwork of Kashmir's
women artisans. I hope you will kindly
accept it and convey best
wishes from the brave daughters of Kashmir
            to the brave daughters of Turkey.
I also hope Turkey undoubtedly supports
our right to determine our
destiny ourselves. We have been fighting
            since long for our freedom. We
thank you and your country for the goodwill
you have shown. Yours faithfully, Mrs.
Maryam Jan. "Katrina," Pindi Point, Murree.

Country Men

Turkish Embassy, Karachi 17 May, 1958

Mrs. Maryam Jan, "Katrina," Pindi Point,
Murree, West Pakistan. Dear Madam,
I am in receipt of your letter dated
          17 April and of the lovely gift
you have been so kind to send me on behalf
of yourself and the women artists
of Kashmir. The workmanship of the jewel case is
          indeed a fine example of skill.
My warmest appreciation for your kind
thought sending this token of regard
the women of Kashmir have for my country
          men. Please accept my sincere wishes
for prosperity of the people of Kashmir,
which, I assure you, is wholeheartedly
shared by the people of Turkey. Faithfully,

General Muzaffer Goksenin, The Ambassador.

Mother Writes to Indira Gandhi

The Hon'ble Mrs. Indira Gandhi,
Prime Minister, Murti Lane, New Delhi,
7 July, 1975, Dear Madam,
      How are you? What's with this
      Emergency? India's star is
fading while you're sexing guru Brahmachari.
A pilot *bucklemeups* in his *sexjet*.
      Pompous rogue has intensified
      wireless, whispering, murmuring:
shanti, ashanti. Indira Ji, please heed my plea:
empty the sky. Show your ire. Command him
      at once ceasefire. A woman's
      mind is no man's land. I hang
my *vaginarags* out on a string — pale buntings
fluttering Kashmir's fragrant breeze. My
      husband remarried. She burps, yawns,
      farts, is fertile and thick as two
planks. Will she leave him alone at dawn to write
his diary? Her two readymade children
      call me, Big Mom, *Bahdi Ami*.
      My husband says new wife will be
my caregiver. It's tearing me apart, Madam,
and I'm again losing my mind. Faithfully
      yours, Mrs. Maryam Jan, Raj Bagh
      Srinagar, Kashmir (India).

Indira Gandhi

New Delhi
30 July, 1975

Dear Maryam Jan, I feel elated to pen this letter in my own hand. A woman's mind is no man's land, indeed. Did your husband tell you he was bringing home a new wife? If he did, he has some redeeming qualities. If he didn't, he has humiliated you. I hope you can find it in your heart to forgive him. It would be the right thing to do — hardest thing to do, I'm learning myself. Many say I'm mad. They have no clue about the fine line between madam and madness — you know it better than I ever will. You have your pilot, his *sexjet*. I have my guru who drives me insane. There is an insurgency in my own emergency with the Brahmachari. Indians are unruly. Elite talk only of civil rights. No one thinks of responsibilities. There are no rights without responsibilities. A dose of self-enlightened dictatorship should give India pause. Remember, from one woman to another, hearts are not broken. They are bruised. Yoga heals. Try it. Enjoy the fragrant breeze. Wish I were there. Kashmir is my ancestral home. Yours, Indira.

Azadi Ka Matlab Kya?
(What does Freedom Mean?)

Sheikh Mohammed Abdullah, Lion Of Kashmir,
August, 1994, Dear Sheikh sahib,
      They tell me you are buried
      on the left bank of Naseem
Lake with a view of the Hazratbal shrine, which
you rebuilt, your tomb guarded by India's troops.
      I tell them this represents
      one of those paradoxes
history keeps throwing up: the same people
who jailed you for eighteen years now guard your tomb
      and the same people whose 'Lion'
      you were are disenchanted
with you for selling out to your paymasters
in New Delhi, who now also bankroll your
      son and his — who dare not even
      sigh while troops, safeguarded by
the Syrupy Secularism Act, suppress
a Vale Of Saints. Gone days when the refrain
      Sheikh Mohammed Abdullah,
      answered our sovereign plea
Azadi Ka Matlab Kya? Today's trendy
refrain is *lā 'ilāha 'illā-llāh* — and that
      should make you rise from your grave.
      Faithfully, Maryam Jan, Raj Bagh.

Mother Writes to her Husband's New Wife

Mrs. Tabasum Khan, Raj Bagh, Srinagar,
Kashmir (India). 7 December, 2000,
       Dear Tabasum, my son Farooq
       says his house by the sea belongs to me
       but the glint in his eye reminds me
       of the glint in his father's eye when
he used to say, which wasn't often, I was his only
beloved wife. The rogue who hounded me in Kashmir
has somehow come also here. My son Farooq is
like his father. He could use his high status
       to catch the scamp who defies even
       U.S. laws, digging deeper to find
       more than gold. "Don't treat me like a child,"
       I tell Maria, mumbling maid from Mexico,
who's her own museum, as she ties a bright bib
around my neck. How long shall I bear this circus?
My son Farooq pledged to fly me back to Kashmir,
but I know he's only teasing. "Stay, now you are
       here," he says. "Who's going to care for you
       there in winter, no power, no heat,
       no water. Dal Lake is ice; army
       sharmy everywhere?" I yearn to see
almond trees blooming, my great-great-grandchildren.
I hope you repainted my room in the attic,
installed western-style commode, for I am still head
of my home. All my love all around as always,
       Fondly, Maryam, New Rochelle, New York.

The New Wife Responds

Dear Maryam Jan, I read your letter over
and over again trying my best to read
between the lines. There is so much there.
      Your son Farooq
      is a Rock
      of Gibraltar,
but then you always said you were proud
of all your six children, regardless
of their status, just as I am of
      my son Ali,
      my daughter Camilla,
      my grandchildren.
Before our husband died, he bequeathed
the ancestral home to me. I can't but see it
as a payoff for having served all to the
      extent I could
      with what we had,
      best I knew how.
A widow, our husband sheltered me,
my two children, yourself for over
a generation under one roof. He was
      a good Muslim.
      My son Ali is
      renovating
our home, a separate room for you,
not in the attic, but on the ground
floor, next to mine, with modern fixtures
      for your comfort,
      a non-nattering
      nanny from Nepal,
perhaps as good as your Mexican maid
in New York. We will paint your room
your favorite bright red, fresh

crimson roses
on your nightstand,
for I know how
you love fragrance. Army terrorizes
only the errant, like the rogue
tormenting you for as long as I know.
My son Ali is
a distributor
of gas heaters.
He will install one in your room,
will also install an inverter
to assure constant supply of power.
Your grandchildren,
great-grandchildren
great-great-grandchildren
will shower almond blossoms on you
I am sure. Please come soon. All our love
from all to all at once. Fondly, Tabasum.
Raj Bagh
Srinagar, Kashmir,
26 January, 2000

Found in Translation

"Give me hair dye," Mother says.
Harry the shrink strokes his beard,

"I'm proud of it," he says.
"Operation doctor sahib,"

She points to the mole on her nose.
"God's gift," he says. She shows him

her ulna fractured in a recent fall.
"Make it as it was."

Harry the shrink displays his bruised wrist,
"Fell off the bike when I was young."

She removes her slip-ons: girl's feet,
red polish chipped at cuticles.

"Slice off my bunions."
Harry the shrink removes his socks,

exposing big misshapen toes.
Mother glares at me, reclined

as usual on the couch,
translating Urdu. "What

does this decrepit man know?
My life is ahead of me."

Starting my Descent

After a bomb rips the baggage claim
I sprout wings running on the tarmac.
Single file khakis blurring smashed
gold of mustard flowers. My legs

collapse. I roar over tips of poplars, follow
the Jhelum upstream where Mother
kneeling at the river's source tears open
a pomegranate with bare hands. "Rubies

from my dowry stolen by the in-laws."
Her *dupatta* undulates and she floats away
reclined on the veil. I give chase, soaring
above the Himalayas, depression fuming

over the Pacific. I am the pallor of twilight
starting my descent. A sign rises to greet me —
The Gilded Cage For The Deranged.
"Wait," a nurse says as I search for Mother.

"Why aren't you already where you're going?"

Two Proposals 60 Years Apart

1938

She circles the room,
the two men cross-legged
on woven flowers,

her kohl-lined eyes downcast
to her shining sandals
at the fringes,

the fluted foot
of a samovar, henna
petals on her toes.

"Look, my child has no flaws,
no need to give ear to rumours,"
her father tells the intended

father-in-law
who's in Srinagar for the viewing,
months before the wedding.

Intended father-in-law —
an expert *d' Objets d' art* —
shakes her father's hand, deal-sealed.

He gives her filigreed silver
wedged heels with pointed tips,
too big for the girl she was,

bunions not yet formed.

1998

Again I ease her palm into mine
we stroll the beach

Frangipani petals
rushlight

inks of her sarong
my bruised jeans

gods on horses
spark the horizon

it's a sign I know
What sign?

Marry me!
Ask me again —

She jolts me
and yet once more

her gritty palm is mine
bending a knee I ask:

Will every flower from
Kenya to Kashmir bloom?

Interweb

for Joyce Maio

From: Linda@coolmaildotcom
"Dreamed about you and Sarah.
Never thought I'd miss you.
Thanks for watering the palm."

From: Sarah@hootmaildotcom
"Bought you the perfect jumper.
It's Cashmere, large, maroon.
The best is yet 2B."

I float up Broadway
to tend to Linda's palm.
Kneeling by her kitchen island
last year I said: "Marry me."

Had she been cooking sole
in the juice of tangerines?
"Oh dear. How odd.
No, for the time being."

To: Sarah@hootmaildotcom
"Yearn for your hugs, luv."
To: Linda@coolmaildotcom
"Chill out. Palm alive."

She Drives as I Scribble on London

The best view is from the Waterloo Bridge
Hope this isn't a bloody one-way street
I wear my French bodice and you don't even notice
My bones rattled when I was anorexic
I skipped rope with the cook's daughter in Mombasa
People are starving because the grain fattens cows for McDonald's
I cannot bear the thought of dead meat in my stomach
You're so ungrateful
I have to buy my own wedding ring?
I understand the offside rule in football better than most men
I didn't want to tell you but I will tell you
When I am premenstrual I smash glass
I don't want a dowry — that's so Asian
London is a city of roundabouts
This is not New York: we give way to other drivers
I never ever indulge in malicious gossip
Will you still hug me after we're married?
We have our demons

A Wife to her Husband

for Tabish Din

This to-ing and fro-ing is but fashion.
You're in Manhattan, I London.
Love can endure a porcelain ocean.

Merely a Kashmiri-Yank, you're torn
(admit it!) in two. I'm a Kenyan-born
Brit, play my own sage, reap what I sow.

Isn't that why you fell for me?
I don't need a Svengali.
If I win, I win. If I lose, I win.

Come, let's grow old in Dublin.

Veracity

after Naserddin

"May I borrow your donkey?"
a neighbour asked Kavanagh

who said, "I'm very sorry,
I loaned out my donkey yesterday."

At that moment, the donkey brayed
in the barn. The neighbour, believing

the donkey made Kavanagh a liar,
asked "Then what is that I hear?"

Kavanagh replied, "Friend, are you going
to believe me or a donkey?"

Assignment

for Marie Howe

Only Muslim in the workshop
I went on a bit about
shock and awe attack on Iraq
weapons of mass destruction
axis of evil
mobile chemical labs
slam dunks
curveball
smoking guns
mushroom clouds
cakewalks
liberators
regime change
and Mission Accomplished.

Civilization's cradle,
I said, is a broken country.
I am a witness
I must howl.
In every well in Baghdad
a *rafiq* is weeping
while long black coats
(with gas masks)
huddle at the Wailing Wall
as if prayers could halt
smart bombs.

"Rhetoric, not lyric,"
my peers echoed Yeats.
"Argue with yourself not others,"
an adjunct admonished, adding
"A warhead soaring
from the earth's womb
was over the top. Navy Seals
stockpiling kneepads was sick.
Not *ars poetica.*"

After Seeing Caryl Churchill's *Seven Jewish Children, A Play for Gaza*

Tell her the proper name of things
this is barbed wire
this is a watch-tower
these are thermal imaging video cameras
these are 25-foot-high concrete slabs
Don't tell her this is a fence
tell her it is a wall

Teach her to spell a p a r t h e i d

Tell her about nukes in the Negev
tell her history's most persecuted minority
a specious democracy in the Middle East
the colonial-settler state embracing biblical pretensions
is systematically exterminating
the world's most dispossessed tribe
"victims of the victims"

Tell her the truth so she grows up to speak its name

Israeli Patrols Kill 90 Dogs in Arab Town
The New York Times, April 14, 1995

Mother, I'm living in sin with an Egyptian
Jew raised in Paris. We stroll in Central Park,
her mutt, Gaulois, off the leash. Lucky he's not
in Hebron, where gods kill dogs for sport.

Rant

for Brian Drolet

America
Now is the Summer of our Discontent
banned bombs
once again rain down
on the world's largest open-air prison
Raggedy Ann dolls pulled out
from Gaza's debris make
even steeliest men sob

America
you arm a colonial settler state
inserted into Palestine
by imperial design
your cop on the beat in the Mid East
assures oil flows like honey
and despots keep subjects quiet

America
when will you give up your oil habit
your whorish bond
with the world's most retrogressive
sexually transmitted dynasty
perfectly disorientated in time, place, person
which pays cash for your Hell-Fire missiles
uses petrodollars to proselytize
a rigid Islam even I don't know?

America
it saddens me
so many bright people don't get
the symbiotic link
between Western Imperialism
and the wretched of the world

It's the New Cold War: their
secular opposition
your imperial despotism
your suppression campaigns
your military henchmen
your gendarme state

America
you say Eisenhower Doctrine
they say Imperial Pillage
it's just dandy, then, to promote
shoe, underwear, flight school
amateur chemistry kids
as Soldiers of Al-Qaeda
"Home-Grown Terrorists"
sworn to destroy
the manicured homeland

America
theirs is a forceful yearning
for Justice
a plea to the human within us
they're holding up a mirror
for you to glance at yourself
America
will you please begin
to see the afterglow
of your empire

"History's Most Persecuted Minority is Insensitive to the Aspirations of the World's Most Dispossessed Tribe."

As Farooq drove in soft rain through red lights to Maimonides, my sister-in-law, Farida, and I sat in the back seat of the sky blue Volkswagen bus. "Kicking," she said placing my hand on her round belly. Shy, I gazed at her polished toes in flip-flops. A stork

dropped a boy in Brooklyn eight years to the day JFK was slain in Dallas. New alien in New York, I babysat my curly-haired nephew in a stark rental on Park Avenue, where the doorman first thought of us as the move-in guys, and where our Numdha rugs, hand-

made in Kashmir, screamed to come out of our walk-in closets. "Make money fast carpeting America from sea to shining sea," Grandfather had penned on an aerogramme. Farooq rode the IRT to Pine Street; Farida was a cashier at Korvettes.

The boy and I together discovered Big Bird on a Zenith console, my first TV exposure at age 22. I watched the boy dunk hoops in Perturbia, his long hair swishing to Metallica's "Disposable Heroes," hunted jack rabbits upstate, enrolled in the local chapter of

the NRA, his dad's rifle on the boy's shoulder. He climbed a peak one summer in Kashmir, a paradise in pathos, a heated topic at our dinner table, but on the periphery of America's mind, rarely mentioned on the *Evening News*, never on *All in the Family*, hit

sitcom that dared to shake America's somnolence even as napalm rained on South East Asia, fueling our rage. In our hearts we knew we had to do what we could with what we had to help untie the Gordian knot of the Kashmir dispute, never again to let mad men

tear apart husbands from wives, siblings from one another, sons and daughters from mothers and fathers, heartbreaks our own family, one of millions, endured on both sides of the Line of Control ever since India divided herself, and I can imagine how this history seized my nephew's receptive mind as he and his mates chilled every Sunday at the Islamic Cultural Center on California Road in Eastchester, once a Greek Orthodox Church, now embraced as house of worship by a fresh wave of immigrants eager to learn

new ways of seeing and thinking. Parents, eager to impart their cultural heritage to their American-born kids, seemed unconcerned as weekday shop owners moonlighted as Sunday school scholars unable to equate the paradox of America's ample prosperity at

home with its wanton supremacy abroad. The shop owners grasped only the literal value of the 72 Virgins in Paradise, urging my nephew to shame his sister for wearing leotards to the ballet class she loved, and to sway his dad to stop serving liquor at home, and yet

they taught him to learn the Call to Prayer which he recited aloud at an annual apple picking party, a holy ritual on a crisp autumn day made me gloomy, for I like my cider with a splash of vodka.

I remember standing next to friends in single line amidst a row of trees, facing East, the women in bright outfits at the rear. Children ran from tree to tree with glee, munched forbidden fallen fruit. Sunrays pierced abundant boughs. I remember being high on aroma.

Apples have mapped the fate of mankind, after all.

Farooq plucked his boy from Perturbia High, enrolled him into High Prep, hoping the good schooling Christian Brothers had drummed into himself when Farooq was a lad growing up in Kashmir would shape the apple-of-his- eye as well. The Brothers cored.

I am struck by the eloquence of this prose poem's title, copied here from my nephew's senior year essay, sealing his fate to the most compelling moral issue of our generation. He was enraged as I, you, we, us should be. How do middle-class Muslim youth from Seattle to Srinagar manage, to the extent they do, their blind rage at the organized ethnic cleansing of Palestinians by Zionists, aided by the world's mightiest democracy? And just as his rage was raw, so is mine. And his rage showed, or perhaps it was a freak accident as he totaled a Toyota

on the Bronx River Parkway, walking away from the wreck, his sack of bones intact, made a U at McGill U, flew to Faisal U, seeking Islam in the Land of the Pure. "We shall meet again," he wrote, "on Judgment Day."

So, April is indeed the cruelest month. Taliban... err... sorry... Mujahedeen... "moral equivalent of the Founding Fathers" an honorific bestowed on them by Ronald Regan, who in turn was dubbed by Gore Vidal, "cue-card-reader President" ... Mujahedeen had taken Kabul.

It was the best of times, it was the worst... a spectacle unfolded. The Mujahedeen, led by a certain Osama Bin Laden, ostracized by his Saudi tribe, trained by the CIA, hunted by the FBI, armed by western capitalist gunrunners, had driven the Soviets out.

What happened to my nephew, what makes sense? I imagine the tall, bearded boy in red and white plaid shirt, slim blue Levis, and a handful of his close classmates, driving a rented Toyota pickup on Asian Highway One. I imagine them crossing the porous

Durand Line to see first-hand the *tamasha*. I imagine them trapped in a firefight between two factions of the Taliban. Wrong time. Wrong place. I imagine infernal arcs across a cobalt sky. I imagine a hurried mass grave near Torkham, Afghanistan.

In New Rochelle, under a gun-metal sky in April, my sister-in-law, Farida, was pruning roses the day the call came.

Appetites

after Rumi

Will bring you figs in bed
come to you as clouds
gradually discover the moon
unstring you knot by knot
feast with you on the roof
weave you out of yourself
uncork your drunkenness
into cups made from skulls
wrap you in a robe of words
chew on your spicy locks
as sometimes in the madhouse
men gnaw on their chains

When I Ask

How does it rain?
You rap a bead of sweat on your forehead

How does lighting strike?
You glance at me and lower your eyes

How does day meet night?
You veil your face with hair

Where does music get its magic?
You lace your talk with honey

What good is yearning?
You snuff a candle with your robe's hem

On Seeing a Sepia Print of Bahadur Shah Zafar, the Last Mughal Emperor

The king is a subject
a world is reversed

gaunt in white
kurta and pajamas

bolstered on a charpoy
long stem of hookah

a humid verandah
garrison in Delhi

banished from the Red Fort
exposed for a Viceroy's pleasure.

Yesterday — seems ages ago — painters
painted his portrait for posterity

slithers of their brush created a halo
above his crown "God's Shadow"

honorifics
cross-legged regalia

woven gardens
blooming beneath feet

subjects trembling
in front of him as they had

in front of his father and his
the garden ravaged

Zafar a memory of his splendor
his sigh's restraint itself a sigh

Old Forms will not be Entertained
(A sign at the Consulate of India, New York)

for David Barsamian

Old chants to the Ganges shall not be entertained
Dead cows float in holy water unrestrained

Family roots shall be ascertained
Nationality of mother should reign

Old friends shall not be entertained
I pledge allegiance to the nuevo-famed

Object of journey shall be explained
To find out etymology of Kashmir-curfewed

Old profession shall not be entertained
Shall I reincarnate as Poet-un-Chained?

An old form (in triplicate) shall be obtained
First copy drained, second birdbrained, third scatterbrained

Enemy passports will be stamped Foreordained
Will heart-rending appeals ever be sustained?

Alternative gods shall be deported
Against the ruins of a world what is regained?

Reading *Lolita* in Kashmir

for Alfred Corn

A boy, I stole
into grandpa's study.

An art dealer,
he loved books

with gilded edges,
Aristotle to Zola

all stuck together
in the humidity.

I snuck Lo out
to his black Chevy

rifled for dirty bits,
steering her away for a spin,

teen-tunes swirling in my head,
I Want to Hold Your Hand.

We hovered over a valley ringed
by sharp mountains, white turbans

on peaks. Lake Dal in the hem,
polished by a soft breeze.

A paisley-shaped river
sobbed through a dazed valley.

Amputated tree trunks screamed
reams of plastic choked icy streams

barbed wire hedged the Shalimar
Toyotas jammed the bazaars.

An ancient Sufi shrine oddly gutted
its rich latticework lost.

New architecture
showed no awe for Nature.

Half-widows wailed
clawed at mass graves

yearning for their disappeared.
Nightingales sang

of joy, not sorrow.
At Zero Bridge

lilacs by bunkers bloomed.
A Lord of the Skies sound-boomed —

startled, stray dogs howled.
In Grandpa's shiny Chevy,

Lolita slipped
from my lap

as we finished
our foreboding odyssey.

Halcyon Day

Two brothers unlike each other

under the copper beech
impatiens bloom on a garden chair

It is going to be a bad day

The only wind is our breathing
Patronizing the silence he says

You've inherited Mother's madness

Better a Dog than Younger Brother

— Persian proverb

When did I begin to see
a father figure? It wasn't
an endearment, shining shoes
for Farooq, my brother.
Daring shaped his character.

I couldn't call out his name.
"We don't address our fathers,"
Harry the shrink said, "by their
first names. Banish fear. Erase
your ego. A seed mingles

into dust before blooming
into a flower. Farooq
can't help but see you
as a kid brother, write you
off as a disaster.

Love your mother; forgive
your father for taking
a new wife younger than
your sister. Your world's vast.
Plumb your own continent."

Carpe Diem

for Agha Ashraf Ali

You light a candle,
carp the darkness,

with your usual flourish
debone a carp,

add a pinch of salt
in your carpeted kitchen

discourse on the next course
to scrape or not the fish head

Gaadkalley: honorific,
you offer a scrap of history,

bestowed once by the people
on the Big Crap who betrayed them.

We seize the head
before the diem carpe us

and raise our glass
to the disappeared carpenters

of Kashmir
a parched paradise.

On Receiving Father at JFK after his Long Flight from Kashmir

As I fling my arms wide, he extends his hand.

Fire Tree

Tips of his mustache whip braided,
a turbaned invader four centuries ago
carried Persian saplings in a caravan
across the Himalayas to Kashmir.

"Our *chinar* will last a thousand years,"
my grandfather said as rustling boughs
reigned above the tin roof of the house
where I was born a Scorpio at midnight.

Every fall each leaf burst into a flower.
We gathered the remains of dyes
to create our rustic fuel for winter,
sprinkling water on burning leaves

palms brushing light ashes together.
I packed fragile coal in a clay pot
matted in painted wicker, my *kangri*,
cloaking it between my knees

under a loose mantle, my *pharun*.
The ashes warmed my bag of bones.
I flew to the future of other worlds,
returning years later to see my father,

sun-withered, sipping his morning tea
alone beside an amputated trunk.
Last night I dreamt I went to Kashmir again.
I was being rowed in an embroidered *shikara*

to the Garden of Rajas who had vanished.
The garden was a sea of hell; our tin roof
collapsed, our fire tree submerged, and
barrenness had become a thousand things.

Passivity

Two Birds of Paradise
on the Tree of Life
dazzle the wall above
his king-size bed

He names the female bird
after my cousin Sofia
heartless tease at fourteen
I too fancy her

feigning sleep in his bedroom
on a corner chaise
my fingers tremble
above combed fringes

Perched on a branch
the male yearns for flight
his one-eyed gaze fixed
upon Grandfather's hand

fondling Sofia on the bed
the female flutters in midair
plumes fanning out
brilliant madder dyes

To Tariq, Younger Brother
7 November, 1952 – 7 November, 2014

The root of our life, the life below the life. — Richard Howard

At Raj Bagh Cemetery

Aha! There you are buried at Father's feet,
next to Uncle Rasool. Are you still
not talking to him? Why did you steer clear

of him all your adult life? Grudges?

We lived our childhood with his children, after
all. Say, "Hello! Uncle Rasool," or your
typical "Howdy!" Believe me, talking cures.

"I don't want to see your face again,"

you wrote me once I sold you my share in
Jewel House for a brotherly sum.
Net one-eighty. In no time, you seeded

Mia's young mind with poison talk: "Don't

trust our family," you told her. "Have faith in
only the peerless Mister Peer, best
friend" — who, by the way, was not at your burial.

Everyone is corruptible,

his creed, you told me once. No money for your
school, you wrote Mia. She spread the news:
I had taken all. Tsk! Tsk! I know no dad,

except in fiction, who would disgrace

his sole heir, not even the tuk tuk driver
who dodges rogue traffic to wheel me
to the lively veggie bazaar at Dal Gate.

Such malice! Matched only by your ex-

wife's mediocrity, turning up her fatuous
nose as if her kind had all the world's
culture, Kashmiris only agriculture.

"I am here," she said at the burial

"to protect my daughter." "From whom?" I asked. She
smiled slyly. Oh, the smell of money!
You lived large from Santa Fe to Srinagar,

left behind a trail of cash deposits,

swept away by your ex, using Mia's
legal shield. You buggered away
your hopes in vile deeds: Sham documents, forged

land records, post-dated checks on closed

accounts, fake currency. No will. No goodwill.
No good faith. Mia inherited
your quirky gene: "Tariq is survived by his

mother, who lives in New York," she said

in a legal brief. "Your niece misled the court
by implication," my lawyer said.
"Not to object will also implicate five

surviving siblings." Monumental

insincerity. It is well past one hundred
eighty days: our handshake deal unsealed.
Shall Mia grow up grasping wicked values,

or embrace fair-mindedness? Is she

filling a bucket at the School of Mercy,
or lighting a fire? No one in this
conceited town will grab her birthright as long

as I am securing mine, unless,

of course the peerless Mister Peer taints
my attorney, or even the judge.
Shall her soul find peace doing it all her way,

tutored by her mother and her crooked

connections? Or shall Mia be guided by
the *Hadith*? "It's a sin," Prophet
Mohammed, peace be upon Him, said, "to take

what is not yours, but it's a bigger

sin <u>not</u> to take what is yours." What would you
know about the *Hadith*? It ain't Sin-
atra. Relatives you shunned arranged a fond

farewell. Stepbrother Ali — Oh how

you hated calling him a stepbrother; loathed
him for looting your rug shop years back
at Father's urging because he unearthed funds

you embezzled from Decorative

Furnishings. Ali lifted your hard hulk, robed
in white, on his broad shoulders. "The past
is the past," stepbrother said, his head held high.

The truth is a terrorist, Tariq.

A divinity measures our deeds. She put
you on the Fast Track queue. The sea was
sympathetic. Disgorged you a day after

a rip-tide lashed you from Calangute

Beach on your sixty-third birthday. Your desire
not to see my face ever again
became your destiny. I saw your bloated face

in a trashy Goa morgue, claimed your corpse,

booked your remains as cargo on a hopping
Air India flight to bury you here.
I wasn't expecting hell on my sixty-sixth birthday.

At Jewel House with Aslum, Older Brother

Aha! Call to Prayer At Dusk, all at once
from banks of the Jhelum and beyond,
a signal for Aslum and me to unscrew

Double Horse whisky. The paint is peeling

in the living room after past September
flood. Some say a chopper plucked you from
the attic. Others, you rafted to safety.

Don't know whom to believe anymore.

A Bill Blass chain-stitch ribbon rug blends suitably
with the steam-cleaned couch. Art-Deco hearth
is ice. In the dining room, *Poppies*

mural by Suzanne is a fading memory.

"Jewel House was bought in the nineteen-twenties
by our Grandfather," Aslum says,
savouring his drink, "from the Maharaja

of Kashmir, who had it dotingly

built for daughter of Nizam of Hyderabad,
richest motherfucker in the Raj" —
a myth you created. As the whisky

loosens him, Aslum describes how he

caught his ex-wife red-handed in "a playful
posture" — his phrase — with Father on his
double bed. "Next day, I told her to get out,"

he slurs. I love discovering Aslum

for the first time in my life. The bond is rich.
Wish you were here, Tariq, your name is
a good word. Aslum and I sip our morning

tea on the verandah, just as you

and I used to do in our dressing gowns, striped
night suits. Red poppies sway near the black
wrought iron gate, my name repainted under

yours. The garden, still damp, is raring

for a haircut as are the evergreens by
the driveway. Broken bricks are scattered
along freshly rebuilt boundary walls. On our

western front, all is loud: the Member

of Parliament is raising a new storey
on his security barracks. Hmm…
did he obtain the required building permit?

On our eastern border, the Police

Officers' Mess is still pinching our electrical
wires. I shall sort that out tomorrow.
When electricity is purloined, power

corrupts. A crimson rose bloomed. Swallows

vie with sparrows over last night's rice Aslum
tossed on the lawn. A nightingale is chirping,
Hello! Hello! Uncle Rasool. Hello!

Geography

"Where are you from?"
I'm often asked
"Manhattan," I answer.

Or I play it straight.
"From Kashmir."
"Is that where wool comes from?"

Sometimes I say, "Exit 18,
M1. Hang a right." In the Himalayas
my roads diverged.

O Blow-In,
outsider in a land of insiders,
embrace the craic.

Not, where are you from,
but where are we going
together?

NOTES

P. 9   *K2*: Second highest peak in the world.

         Eid al-Adha: One of Islam's most sacred days. To establish centrality for Ishmael (Father of the Arab nation), Muslims say it was he — not Isaac — whom God had asked Abraham to sacrifice. The day is marked by festivity and sacrifice of goats and lambs.

         Bismillah: In the name of Allah.

P. 10-12   *Shalimar:* Famous Mughal garden in Srinagar, the summer capital of Kashmir.

P. 14   Inspired by "I Go Back to May 1973" by Sharon Olds.

P. 15-17   *Ceasefire Line or Cease Fire Line:* Now called The Line of Control.

P. 20   Inspired by "The Hanging Man" by Sylvia Plath.

P. 21-22   *Ativan and Zyprexa*: Anti-anxiety and anti-psychotic drugs, respectively.

P. 25-26   *Champion Lovemaker*: In Sufism, endearing term for the Prophet Mohammed.

         Nikab: A veil for the face that leaves the area around the eyes clear. It is worn with an accompanying headscarf.

P. 34   *Indira Ji*: Sounds like Madam G, a form of respect for Mrs. Indira Gandhi, former Prime Minister of India.

         Emergency: In India, "the Emergency" refers to a 21-month period in 1975-77 when Prime Minister Indira Gandhi unilaterally had a state of emergency declared across the country.

         Brahmachari: Reportedly, during the Emergency Mrs. Gandhi was having an affair with Dhirendra Brahmachari, her Yoga teacher.

         Shanti: Peaceful; *Ashanti*: Turmoil.

P. 36   This became the defining slogan of the popular insurgency that erupted in 1989 in Kashmir, encapsulating years of disenchantment against Indian rule. The rhyming refrain, *lā 'ilāha 'illā-llāh (There is no god but God)* embraced Islamic resurgence after the Taliban, aided by a Western coalition, drove the Soviets out of Afghanistan. During the preceding fifty-two years the slogan rhymed with the refrain *Sheikh Mohammed Abdullah*: 1905-1982, one of the most important political figures in the modern history of Kashmir. Pandit Nehru, India's First Prime Minister and father of Indira Gandhi, jailed the Sheikh for eighteen years for demanding self-rule for Kashmir.

lā 'ilāha 'illā-llāh: *There is no god but God:* The defining creed of Muslims, a statement of both ritual and worship. In the *Hadith* (the sayings of Prophet Mohammed) Angel Gabriel defines Islam to Mohammed that he should "witness there is no god but God."

P. 41   *Dupatta*: A veil.

P. 47   Adapted from a humorous tale, *Whom do you Believe?* by Naserddin Hodja, a satirical Sufi, believed to have lived and died during the 13th century in today's Turkey. He is considered a populist philosopher and wise man, remembered for his funny anecdotes.

P. 48   *Rafiq:* A friend in Arabic; a companion of the journey in Farsi.

P. 49   A major playwright in the tradition of Bertolt Brecht and Samuel Beckett, Caryl Churchill has won several awards. The play was penned and staged in response to Israel's brutal massacre in Gaza. "Operation Cast Lead," Israel's carefully calculated and long-planned 22-day December '08/January '09 attack on Gaza, resulted in the deaths of 1,300 Gazans, the majority unarmed civilians, and left communities in shambles.

P. 51-52 Inspired by Allen Ginsburg's "America"(*Howl and other Poems*, 1956, City Lights).

P. 53-55 *Maimonides*: Hospital in Brooklyn named after famous Jewish scholar.
     IRT: Inter Rapid Transit.
     Numdah: Felt rugs.
     Korvettes: A long defunct chain of department stores.
     NRA: National Rifle Association.
     April is the cruelest month: From "The Wasteland" by T.S. Eliot.
     72 Virgins in Paradise: The Qur'an states that all Muslim males, not only martyrs, will be rewarded with virgins in Paradise. This has led to the 72 Virgins concept being used as a way to entice young Muslims into martyrdom for Islam.
     Land of the Pure: Pakistan.
     Durand Line: The long border between Afghanistan and Pakistan established in 1893 by agreement between Sir Mortimer Durand and

civil servants of British India and Abdur Rahman Khan, the Afghan Amir, to fix the limit of their respective spheres of influence.
Tamasha: A fuss or commotion.

P.58   *Bahadur Shah Zafar* (1775-1862): Mughal Emperor exiled by the British to Ragoon in Burma after the 1857 Indian mutiny. Prior to defeating him in battle and imprisoning him, the British East India Company reduced Zafar and his family to a state of dependence. He was also one of the great Urdu poets of India.
Kurta: A collarless, loose-fitting sheer cotton shirt.
Charpoi: An improvised bed made of wood planks.

P. 60-61   *Dal Lake*: A shrinking lake in Srinagar.
Zero Bridge: Historically, nine bridges span the Jhelum in Srinagar. In the 1960's when a new bridge was located before the First Bridge, it was named Zero Bridge in order to keep the historical sequence, from one to nine, intact. Now, new bridges are named after politicians.

P. 64   *GaadKalley:* Head of a fish, in Kashmiri, or Fish Head. The reference is to Sheikh Mohammed Abdullah: 1905-1982. See note above under 'Azadi Ka Matlab Kya?'
Sheikh Abdullah was endowed with a big head, or, metaphorically, his head was in the clouds.

P. 66   *Chinar:* Kashmir's plane tree. *Chi* means tree in Farsi, *Nar* fire.
Kangri: also known as *kangar* or *kangri* is a (clay) pot filled with hot embers used by Kashmiris beneath their traditional clothing to keep the chill at bay, which is also regarded as a work of art.
Pharun: Traditional loose cloak worn by Kashmiris during the winter months.
Shikara: A boat similar to a gondola, decorated with hand-embroidered crewel fabric cushions and curtains.

P. 68-73   *The root of our life, the life below the life:* A line by Richard Howard from his poem "Wildflowers"(*Selected Poems*, Penguin Books, 1991). Used with the permission of the author.
Hadith: The sayings of Prophet Mohammed.

P. 74   *Blow-In:* Slang for new immigrants to Ireland.
The "Craic": Irish for fun, enjoyment.

ACKNOWLEDGEMENTS

Acknowledgements are due to the following publications in which versions of some of these poems first appeared: *With Eyes Wide Open: Poetry for the New American Century* (West End Press, 2014); *Ravishing Disunities: Real Ghazals in English (Wesleyan Poetry Series, 2000)* by Agha Shahid Ali and Sarah Suleri Goodyear; *Tin House; Quarto Literary Magazine of Columbia University; The Asian Pacific American Journal; The Irish Examiner;* and *3 QuarksDaily.com.*

'Hallucinations' was performed on stage by the Columbia University Dramatic Club in Fall 1999.

And, for the usual and unusual reasons, many thanks to Farooq and Farida Kathwari, Tabish Din, Mohammad Tabish, Agha Shahid Ali, Colette Inez, The Patrick Kavanagh Center and Brian Lynch, John Walsh and Lisa Frank of Doire Press, and last but not least, Susan Shapiro and her incomparable Tuesday Night Writing Workshop, held at her home in Manhattan's West Village, where over ten years I first plumbed these poems from my depths.

RAFIQ KATHWARI is the first non-Irish recipient of the Patrick Kavanagh Poetry Award, in the forty four-year history of the award. He lives in Ballyoonan (Baile Uí Mhaonáin), County Louth, but has lived most of his adult life in New York. Born, as he puts it, "a Scorpio at midnight" in the disputed Kashmir Valley, Rafiq has translated from the original Urdu selected poems of Sir Mohammed Iqbal, one of the handful of great South Asian poets of the 20th century writing in Urdu. He obtained an MFA in Creative Writing at Columbia University and a Masters in Political and Social Science from the New School University. He divides his time between New York City, Baile Uí Mhaonáin and Kashmir. *In Another Country* is his debut collection.